SPACE EXPLORATION and TRAVEL

Troll Associates

SPACE EXPLORATION and TRAVEL

by Louis Sabin

Illustrated by Holly Moylan

Troll Associates

Library of Congress Cataloging in Publication Data

Sabin, Louis.
    Space exploration and travel.

    Summary: Briefly traces the history of space flight
and explains how satellites and other spacecraft move
through space.
    1. Space flight—Juvenile literature. [1. Space
flight.   2. Space vehicles]   I. Moylan, Holly, ill.
II. Title.
TL793.S18   1985   629.45   84-2698
ISBN 0-8167-0258-6 (lib. bdg.)
ISBN 0-8167-0259-4 (pbk.)

Human beings have always looked to the skies and dreamed of traveling into space. But until the middle of the twentieth century, space travel remained no more than a dream. Then, on October 4, 1957, *Sputnik 1*, a Russian satellite, was successfully launched. The Space Age had begun.

Since that day, many spacecraft—with and without human occupants—have been sent beyond the Earth's atmosphere. Astronauts have walked on the moon; they have lived in space for weeks at a time; they have linked, or joined, two spacecraft far out in space.

Astronauts also have piloted reusable spaceships and landed them back on Earth, like ordinary jet planes. Space probes without crews have been sent into the far reaches of our solar system to gather information about the most distant planets. Every year brings new advances into the uncharted frontier of the universe.

The first major step in scientific knowledge needed for space travel was made by Johannes Kepler, a German scientist. In the early seventeenth century, Kepler worked out the laws of planetary motion. These laws described the way the planets and their natural satellites, called moons, travel through space.

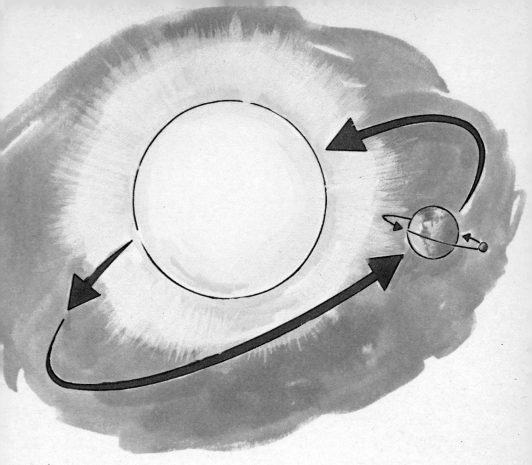

The path planets and moons follow in their travels is called an orbit. An orbit is roughly circular. The Earth travels in an orbit around the sun. And the moon travels in an orbit around the Earth.

Another scientist who provided knowledge necessary for space flight was England's Sir Isaac Newton. Newton contributed the revolutionary theories of motion and gravity. These laws of universal gravitation and motion provided the scientific basis for the development of rockets and orbital travel. But not until 1903 were the ideas of high-powered rocketry and space travel seriously considered.

It was during that year that a Russian, Konstantin Tsiolkovsky, published a technical paper describing how rockets might reach beyond Earth's atmosphere. At the time, however, rocket technology was at a primitive level of development.

Then, in 1926, the first practical break-through occurred when Robert Goddard, an American physicist, invented a rocket that used liquid fuel. It did not fly far or for very long, but it was a great step forward.

During World War II, liquid-fuel-powered rockets were used by the Germans as weapons. After the war, Wernher von Braun, director of the German rocket program, came to the United States to supervise development of its rocket program.

Other German scientists went to Russia to do similar work. Soon a race was underway between the two nations to launch artificial satellites into space.

Since the first successful space launch, in 1957, there have been two forms of space vehicle—those with a human crew and those without a human crew. *Sputnik, Explorer, Vanguard, Luna, Pioneer, Mariner,* and others are spacecraft without a human crew. These vehicles have been put to a variety of uses. In some cases, the flights are like mechanical scouts that check out unknown territory. Only when it has been proven that it is safe for humans to go are flights with crews allowed to follow.

Surveyor 1 and *Surveyor 5* were spacecraft without crews that sent back data from the moon. This data was later used when astronauts were sent to the moon for the first time. Other uncrewed satellites, such as *Voyager 2*, have been sent to explore Saturn, Uranus, and Neptune. These three planets are so far from Earth that astronauts cannot, at present, travel to them and return.

Satellites without crews are also used as permanent orbiting information gatherers. They send back data on such subjects as the Earth's weather, geography, oceans, and volcanic activity. Other satellites are used for communications, including radio, television, and telephone. Signals from Earth are bounced back from these orbiting craft and received in places far from their original sending stations.

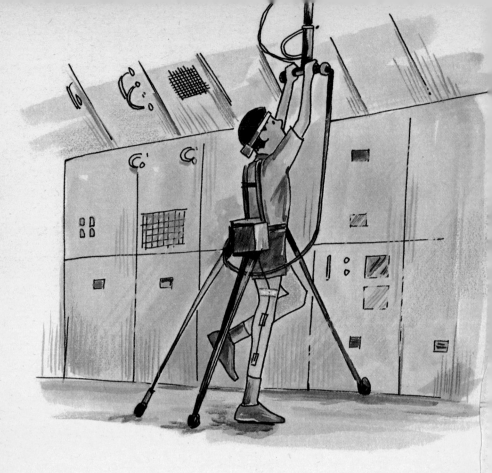

Satellites carrying human crews have traveled to the moon and back. Others have orbited the Earth for days, weeks, even months at a time. During these flights, astronauts test equipment, gather data on many scientific subjects, and study the effects of outer space on people.

A space flight begins when a spacecraft is launched beyond Earth's atmosphere. The main challenge of the launch is overcoming gravity. Gravity is the force that pulls all objects toward the Earth.

In order to overcome the Earth's gravity, the rockets that power a spacecraft must move it at a very high rate of speed. This speed gives the craft enough thrust, or push, to carry it beyond the effect of Earth's gravitational pull.

Much can be learned from sending up
pilotless spacecraft, but there is a limit to the
information that can be gathered this way.
For example, only by sending humans into
space can we determine how space
conditions affect the human body.

The force of the thrust needed to launch a spacecraft places a considerable strain on the human body. This strain increases with the speed of the craft. To counteract the pressure, called g forces, astronauts must wear special, pressurized flight suits. They must also be strapped in a lying-down position on special couches. Lying down and wearing a pressurized suit help to keep an astronaut's heartbeat and blood pressure as close to normal as possible.

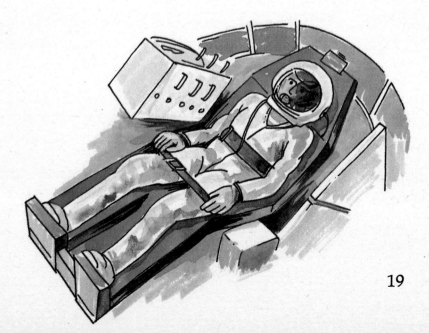

Treadmill exercise

Once a spacecraft is beyond the Earth's atmosphere, gravity is no longer a problem. But in space, everything is weightless. So astronauts must fasten everything down in their space capsule to keep it from floating away. Food must be squeezed from tubes.

And—since there is no gravity—astronauts do not get any exercise from routine movements of their bodies. To stay in good physical shape, they must perform special exercises while they are weightless.

A number of space voyages have included space walks. A space walk is an action requiring an astronaut to work outside the craft. During this time, the astronaut wears a many-layered space suit, which protects the body from the sun's radiation and from particles of space dust called micro-meteoroids.

Space walk

A space-walking astronaut is always attached to the craft by a long, flexible tube. This tube has radio transmission lines and carries oxygen from the craft to the astronaut. Not only does it keep the astronaut breathing and in communication with others, the tube is a life line. If it were cut, the astronaut would drift off into space.

In order to return to Earth, an orbiting spacecraft must be pointed in the right direction and must fire rockets that slow its speed. The slowing allows gravity to pull the craft back toward Earth. As the craft heads back to Earth, parachutes are released automatically. These parachutes help slow the craft even more and steady it. Then the craft floats down to Earth.

The main problem during the return flight of any spacecraft is the heat that builds up as it re-enters the Earth's atmosphere at high speed. This is due to the friction, or rubbing, of the craft against the air it is passing through. All spacecraft are protected against this intense heat by a heat shield. The heat shield of the space shuttle, for example, is made of many ceramic tiles.

On July 20, 1969, the first lunar landing took place. On that occasion, two Americans, Neil Armstrong and Edwin Aldrin, walked on the moon's surface. Their mission was followed by five more United States moon shots.

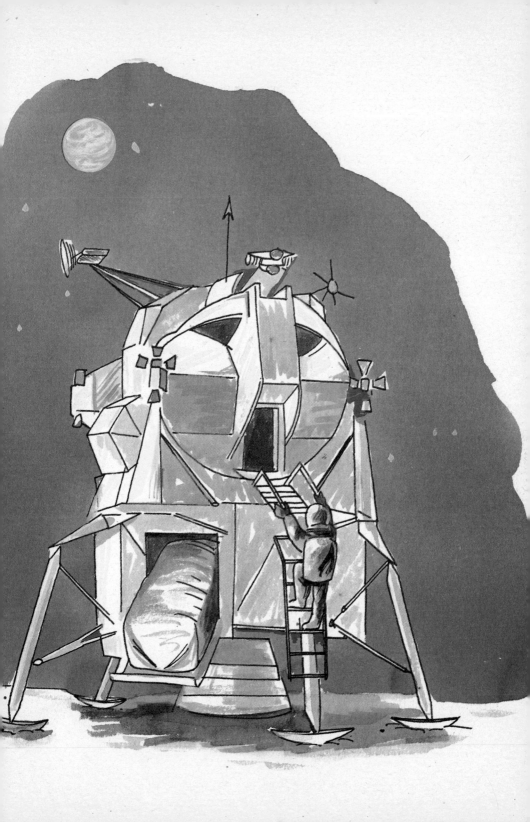

On every American lunar mission, a lunar module made a soft landing on the moon's surface. And each time, astronauts set up scientific equipment and carried out scientific experiments.

When they were finished, they launched their module from the moon and reattached it to the orbiting Apollo spacecraft. Then each mission ended with a return journey to Earth.

The Soviet Union's *Salyut* and America's *Skylab* were designed as orbiting space stations and were used by a succession of teams of astronauts. In these scientific space stations, astronauts studied subjects such as solar radiation and the uses of solar energy.

They also learned a great deal about the effects of prolonged weightlessness on humans. The information they gathered will enable future space voyagers to travel more safely on longer space missions.

The American space shuttle, *Columbia*, made its first voyage in March of 1981. Since then it has been reused a number of times. Each flight brought us closer to the possibility of permanent orbiting space stations and of flight to the stars. And this is just the beginning. Someday great spacecraft may carry humans to other galaxies in the limitless universe around us.